The Girlfriends' Bible

Other Books by Cathy Hamilton

Momisms
Dadisms
Kidisms

THE
GiRL
FRiENDS'
BiBLE

Cathy Hamilton

**Andrews McMeel
Publishing**

Kansas City

The Girlfriends' Bible

04 05 06 07 08 KP1 10 9 8 7 6 5 4 3

ISBN: 0-7407-4341-4

Library of Congress Control Number:
2003112471

Attention: Schools and Businesses

Andrews McMeel books are available at
quantity discounts with bulk purchase for
educational, business, or sales promotional use.
For information, please write to: Special Sales
Department, Andrews McMeel Publishing,
4520 Main Street, Kansas City, Missouri 64111.

For my girlfriends—
past, present, and future.

THE BOOK OF
GENIFER

FEAR not, for I am your girlfriend.

CRY out to me in times of trouble, and I will comfort you with ice cream, liquor, or the sedative of your choice.

WHITHER thou goest, I will go. Whither thou sleepest, I will never tell.

YEA, though you walk through the valley of cracked sidewalks in high heels, do not fear. For I will be there to pick you up when you fall on your ass.

I WILL do unto you as you do unto me. And when you do unto me as I would never dream of doing unto you, I will forgive you, after I curse you and denounce your name.

I SHALL not take thy name in vain. Even when I am enraged with you for standing me up to be with a man or for spilling wine on my favorite silk dress, my tongue shall never be forked.

LEAD me not into temptation and I will endeavor not to lead you.

I SHALT not steal your boyfriend, hairdo, or signature fragrance.

I SHALT not covet your man, clothes, handbags, or shoes. (Or, if I do, I shalt keep my coveting to myself.)

WHOSOEVER may cast aspersions and call you a whore, slut, or fashion victim, shall be wise to fear me. Because I will rise up and lash out at the aspersion caster. For you are my girlfriend and whosoever asperses you, asperses me.

THE BOOK OF BABS

LET me be your rock.

* When your confidence is shaken by nasty rumormongers or jealous ex-boyfriends, come to me and I will build you up again.
* When you are afraid of a blind date, first day on the job, or ob-gyn appointment, I will bolster your courage with feeble pep talks.
* And when Valentine's Day approaches and you have no lover to ply you with flowers, diamonds, or chocolates, call on me and I will console you with encouraging words and rationalizations.

WHEN you come to me seeking the truth about your man, a new haircut, or swimsuit, ye shall know the truth and the truth shall set you free.

CONFIDE in me your secrets and I will take them to my grave. Do not, however, reveal your secrets when I am doused with alcohol or under anesthesia, or all bets are off.

WHEN you find your-
self held in bondage
by a difficult relationship,
dead-end job, or too-tight
leather pants, I will come
to your rescue. And you
shall be released.

AMEN, I say to you! If you desire to go out wearing ripped sweat pants from Kmart and no makeup, I will say "Amen." If you imbibe too much alcohol and dance by yourself on top of a table, I will say "Amen!" If you decide that no amount of money is worth the pain of electrolysis, Sister, I will say "Amen!"

*T*URN to me when you are in need.

❋ When you are moving, I will help you pack and carry.
❋ When you are stranded across town without a car, I will come to your rescue.
❋ When you need a ride to the airport, I will be your chauffeur.
❋ When you're desperate for an excuse to escape a date that's gone horribly wrong, send me a sign and I will call you on your cell and fake a heart attack.

AND when your period hath not cometh and it is, lo, five days, or six, or even a fortnight late, and you are anguished, I will sit with you, and we will watch and wait until the test strip turns blue or pink. And you will know that whatever comes, I will be there for you.

AND if I should win
infinite riches from a
game of chance like the
multistate lottery, I will
share with you my good
fortune and treat you to a
spa vacation or Caribbean
cruise, just as you would
certainly share such riches
with me.

THE BOOK OF
SYBIL

WHEN you are heavy
laden with PMS
poundage, I will take your
burden for you and deny
thy girth.

AND I shall know,
without being told,
that it is that time of the
month for you. And I shall
be not afraid.

IF your hormones run amok and you are plagued by mood swings that cause you to resemble a person with multiple personality disorder, I will not abandon you, but comfort you with calming reassurances, yoga videos, and Prozac. And you shall do the same in return.

AND when your appetite rages out of control, and you crave an abundance of carbohydrates and fats, smothered in a pillar of salt, I shall restrain you until your willpower is restored.

I WILL not be surprised or fearful when you burst into tears without provocation. And you will not be alarmed when I do the same. For we will know that the all-powerful hormones are to blame for our madness. And we will shout at the heavens, raising our fists, and curse the gods of Estrogen, Progesterone, and Testosterone. And this, along with the Prozac, shall give us peace.

KNOW this: When you are in agony because you are plagued by cramps, and these cramps are causing you extreme discomfort, I will share with you my pain medication, without reservation, even if I am down to my last Vicodin. And it will be good.

THE BOOK OF
NICOLE

BE confident of this
very thing: No man,
no matter how handsome,
or wealthy, or hard of
body, shall ever come
between us.

IF there is but one attractive man in a room and the two of us see this man, and we covet this man, and desire to have babes in swaddling clothes with him, I will sacrifice my wants for you . . . but only if you saw him first.

WHEN you have been
mistreated
by boyfriends, bosses,
or bitches, call on me and
we will curse them in the
darkness together.

FOR if you succumb to
temptations of the flesh,
confess your sins to me—
in great detail, holding
nothing back—and I
will not cast stones or rush
to condemn, but comfort
you with tales of my own
juicy indiscretions.

WHEN you need a place to rest and can find no room at the inn, your crowded apartment, or your boyfriend's place, I will give you shelter for the night—unless, of course, I am busy sheltering another needy night visitor.

WHEN it comes to pass that it's New Year's Eve and we lack male companionship but our party dresses are fine, we will dress up and go out and dance until lo' after midnight and escort each other home, hand in hand, and worry not about what others might think.

THE BOOK OF CHRISSIE

*C*OUNT on me in times of turmoil.

WHEN your jeans no longer fit, I will reassure you that your dryer must be too hot.

WHEN the first fine line
appears on your face
and you are overcome
with misery, I will point
out my own fine lines and
the fine lines of other
women your age in order
to ease your pain.

AND when your stylist betrays you with a vile and horrific haircut, and you threaten to go into exile for thirty days and thirty nights, I will come to you bearing wine, chocolate, and an abundance of hats.

THE BOOK OF FERGIE

AND I say unto you,
"Diets be damned!"

FOR when we are invited to a grand feast and there is an abundance of meat, pasta, bread, and wine, and we help ourselves to this bounty and fill our plates upward toward the heavens, I will not remind you of your diet and you will not remind me of mine.

BE not afraid. If you should lose control and go on a never-ending binge following a breakup or similar devastation, it shall be my moral obligation to join you and partake for as long as you partake.

AND, thus, when you lose a monumental, or even trivial, amount of weight, I shall rejoice with you and sing your praises, just like I'd want you to rejoice with me if the circumstances were reversed.

WHEN you break your diet and succumb to gluttony, I will be there to accompany you to the gym and sweat with you until we both lose consciousness.

AND when I have suffered a breakup or similar devastation and I hunger for a binge of gluttony and excess, and I know you are trying to diet, I will refrain from asking you to join me in my recklessness.

AND we shall preach to whoever is willing to listen that Size 0 is not acceptable for people over five feet tall, and that the emaciated urban waif look is so passé as to be criminal. And we shall praise the Zaftig Woman and rejoice in our curves.

THE BOOK OF
YOLANDA

BELIEVE me when I say unto you, if we tread into the troubled waters of a public restroom, desperate to find a stall, and my needs are not as dire as yours, I will let you stand ahead of me in line.

AND if you simply cannot wait for a stall because your needs are too great, I will throw myself on the mercy of the line and beg them to let my girlfriend go.

AND it will come to pass that you find yourself stranded in a restroom stall and, alas, there will be no toilet paper for which to use. Call out to me and I will come to your rescue with not one but several squares.

AND thus we will share equally, and without reservation, all items of personal hygiene and beauty. For my lipstick is your lipstick. My hairbrush is your hairbrush. My tampons are your tampons. (Although this does not mean my *specific* tampons are your *specific* tampons.)

AND if I see something out of place on your person—a stray hair, unzipped fly, or errant shirt tag—I will call your attention to the imperfection, without causing you embarrassment, so that you may rectify it and present your best self, just as you would do in return for me.

THE BOOK OF TIFFANY

*T*HIS is the friendship
Lord and Taylor has
made. Let us rejoice and
be glad for shopping.

WHEREFORE now
this day, I ordain thee
to be the high priestess of
the shopping, and I the
second most high. And
the great aisles of the
store shall part and all
lowly shoppers shall bow
down before us and call
us "Your Highnesses."

L ET us enter the king-
dom of retail and fear
no evil sales clerks, per-
fume squirters, or return
policies. For we will face
them together and rise up
in the face of department
store danger.

*T*HOU shalt not take any man into the misses' department, unless he is gay, for it will be fruitless.

AND we shall obey the Ten Command-
ments of Shopping as if our very lives
depend on them:

✻ One can never have too many black
  shoes, dresses, or pants.
✻ Thou shalt not wear the same outfit
  twice in one workweek.
✻ What sets us apart from the beasts is
  our ability to accessorize.
✻ Stylishness is next to godliness.
✻ Thou shalt not take the name of Ralph
  Lauren in vain.
✻ Honor thy father and thy mother's
  fashion sense. But don't necessarily
  subscribe to it.

�֍ It is a sin to be seen in last season's anything.
�֍ You can find salvation at a sample sale.
�֍ Thou shalt not seek redemption in a designer dress when a perfectly good knock-off will suffice.
✖ The right to return shall be made universal as ordained by the Almighty.

AND we will conduct
ourselves according to
the highest indisputable
law: More is more. And
we will resist the temptation to restrict our buying
simply because we have
no more cash or room in
our closets.

IF there is but one dress or pair of shoes in a department store that you find desirable, and I desire the same dress or pair of shoes, I will forfeit them to you because I am your friend. And because I know you will gladly loan them to me whenever I wish.

AND I tell you this, if
we are shopping and
you find an outfit that
you adore, but that outfit
does not flatter you and,
in truth, makes you look
like a fatted cow, I will
not purchase that outfit
for myself no matter how
much I covet it.

IF your cup runneth over
because your bra is too
small and you look like a
common whore, I will
tell you, just as you would
tell me about visible panty
lines.

AND we shall bid farewell forever to such tragic trends as colossal shoulder pads and sequin-appliquéd wind suits, making believe we never wore them in the first place.

AND when a store clerk asks you what size you are and you answer with the lowest size in your closet, whether you can still squeeze into it or not, I will honor your answer and treat it as the truth.

*T*OGETHER we will
come to know which
merchants use "skinny
mirrors" to deceive
their unsuspecting cus-
tomers, and we will
denounce them and shop
accordingly.

AND we will forsake
fashion convention
and wear white pants *and*
white shoes after Labor
Day if we damn well
please! And it will be
good.

KNOW this: I will not mock you if you surrender to the trend of the moment and show up at an important function in a ridiculous-looking ensemble. Even when others deride you and scorn your fashion sense, I will defend your taste and admonish your critics by explaining that you are on a new medication that greatly impairs your judgment.

AND we will worship the power and glory of shoes, and gaze in awe at the abundance of styles, colors, and heel heights, and thank the Creator for such a wonderful world.

AND I sayeth unto you, if you should darken the door of a discount clothing or knock-off store, I shalt not find fault. For whosoever among us is without guilt of bargain shopping, let her throw the first credit card.

FOR when you succumb in a moment of weakness and impulsively buy something outrageously expensive, thus exceeding your credit card limit and requiring two credit cards, or, heaven forbid, the malevolent layaway, I will not condemn or admonish you, especially if the outfit in question happens to fit me, too.

AND if you need to hide that expensive outfit from your husband or significant other for a period of days, weeks, or months because you fear terrible repercussions, I will hold that outfit for safekeeping until the appropriate time when you can confess your sin. And if, by chance, I happen to have occasion to wear that outfit, I will do so without fearing your wrath because I have done you this magnanimous favor.

IF you come to me in search of a dress, shoes, or jewels to borrow, I will open my door to you and say, "Seek and you shall find." But woe to you if you do not return what you find in one week or less.

THE BOOK OF
MARY KAY

FOR when a cosmetics clerk, whose livelihood depends on commissions, declares that your makeover gives you that Marilyn Monroe look when, in reality, it's more like Marilyn Manson, I will proclaim the ugly truth and drag you by the hair to the nearest ladies' room.

AND we will forsake
blue eye shadow for-
ever, never looking back,
lest we turn into a pillar
of glitter.

BE it ordained that it is our divine right to acquire the free gift at the Clinique counter, with no regard as to how many free gifts we already own nor how much money we have to spend gratuitously to obtain the free gift. Because possessing the free gift is our inalienable entitlement. And it is always good.

AND we shall know, deep in our souls and without a doubt, that one can never possess too many lipsticks. For the shades of lipstick are too plentiful and there is but one color that is predestined for each woman on Earth, and the quest for this perfect color sometimes takes a lifetime.

AND if I should observe
lipstick on your teeth,
I will point it out to you so
that you might rid yourself
of the smear before repuls-
ing someone with your
smile. And you will do the
same for me. And it will
be right.

FOR when I notice a wayward and unwanted chin hair protruding from your face and you cannot see this protrusion, I will call your attention to the hair so that you might pluck it. And you will do the same for me in return. And we shall both be whiskerless.

BE assured that when I observe that you appear tired and haggard and your eyes are puffy and swollen with water retention, I will not ridicule you but recommend, with gentility and kindness, that it's time for a detoxifying facial.

FOR we shall instinc-
tively know when it is
time to sacrifice our fore-
heads to the god Botox.
And we shall hold each
other's hand, and steel
ourselves for the numbing
needle, and not despair
when we cannot show
surprise for ninety days
and nights.

AND if one of us should choose to go under the knife and allow a doctor to lift our face high toward the heavens, the other will not criticize, ridicule, or pass judgment, because heaven only knows when the tables will turn.

THE BOOK OF
Jessica

AND I will say "Yea" and be exceedingly glad when you find a man who comforts, protects, and pleasures you, and I will not feel envy, even if the man is gloriously hot, and I have not had such a man in a very long time.

AND when that man maketh you to lie down in green pastures with him, and it comes to pass that he does *not* perform like manna from heaven, I will leadeth you to the still waters of the nearest pub and drink to your sad misfortune.

AND if, after several unfulfilling couplings, you decide to spare your man's rod and spoil the relationship, I will support your decision because woman does not live on bread alone.

IF I witness your man
coveting another woman,
and you are not there to
witness this for yourself,
I will come to you and
report what I have seen.
For you are my friend,
and he is but a snake in
the grass. And friends are
more righteous than
snakes.

AND if you suspect your man is cheating on you with another depraved woman, and you seek to confirm your suspicion as truth or falsehood, I will drive you in my car past his dwelling, while you hide stealthily on all fours on the floor, and together we will spy, for as long as it takes, to see if he is faithful or a despicable snake.

BE certain of this. If the love of your life jilts you with the age-old pathetic excuse: "It's not you, it's me," I will make it my life's mission to convince you that "Damn right, it's him . . . because you're fabulous!"

LO, and when you have been deeply wronged by a man, and you desire never to see his hideous face again, and you seethe with bitterness, I will come to you and we will drink wine and gather his photos, letters, and ridiculous bikini briefs, and cast them into the burning fire so that his memory will haunt you no more. And we shall toast to your newfound freedom and drink to future photos, letters, and boxer shorts.

SHOULD your man betray you for another, grieve you with his adultery, and abandon you on your darkest day, I shall seek revenge on that man and make him sorry he was ever born of this world.

AND should you betray
your man for another,
I will not cast stones, for
I will know you must have
had a very good reason.

LO, and when I behold
you are ready to
drunk-dial your old flame
because you are con-
sumed with sexual long-
ing and he looks better in
hindsight than he ever did
before, I will stop you and
remind you of his numer-
ous faults and the reasons
you dumped his sorry ass
in the first place.

THE BOOK OF Sadie

FOR when you decide to take a husband in a grand wedding ceremony, I will rejoice and gladly wear the bridesmaid dress of your choosing, no matter how hideous or impractical.

AND I will toast you at your wedding celebration and give a heartfelt speech, never mentioning, no matter how tempted or loose-lipped I am from the wine, how many frogs you had to kiss before you found your prince.

BELIEVE this: I will not reveal the sordid stories of your past, no matter how checkered, to your husband or new in-laws. For you possess as much dirt on me as I possess on you. And I am no fool.

AND when it comes to pass that you decide to be fruitful and multiply with this man, I will support your decision and not tempt you with alcohol, caffeine, or cigarettes.

IF you should become
heavy with child and
your womb starts expand-
ing beyond mortal imagi-
nation, I will reassure you
that you're not that big,
even if it means forsaking
the truth for a moment.

AND when you fear that stretch marks are taking over your body and causing your stomach to look like a roadmap of Jerusalem, I will comfort you with assurances that cropped shirts are too trendy and one-piece swimsuits never go out of style.

WHEN that child is born unto you, and you are overcome with emotion and are distraught because you fear your bosoms will never return to normal, I will point out the normal bosoms of other mothers and restore your hope.

AND when you are weary and bordering on collapse because you have not had a good night's rest since the baby was born, I will come to your rescue and care for your child while you sleep.

AND when you haven't known your husband in the biblical sense for a very long time because you are ready to drop from exhaustion, and you fear that you've forgotten how to perform the marital act, I will console you and remind you of even longer dry spells of involuntary abstinence from your past.

AND when you are overcome with remorse because you question your maternal instincts, all because you failed to wipe off the pacifier after it fell to the floor, I will reassure you that too much sanitation is, in fact, an undesirable thing, and that babies' immune systems need to be exposed to germs. And you will believe.

FOR when you are deeply troubled by your thankless children, and the floodgates open and your tears come flowing down because you are disheartened, call on me and I will come to your aid with an abundance of chocolate, the likes of which you have never seen, and I will listen tirelessly to your tales of woe while we both are suckling on Kahlúa truffles.

The Book of Stella

AND we shall celebrate
each and every birth-
day as if it is our last and
worry not about the day
after.

ND if you or I should move away to another city or town, and this cannot be avoided, I vow to actually keep in touch and not just give it lip service.

FOR no matter how
occupied we become
with jobs, men, children,
or the other concerns of
life, we shall always make
time for female bonding.
For camaraderie is our
light and our salvation,
and is exceedingly
cheaper than therapy.

AND it shall be ordained that "Girls' Night Out" is the sacrosanct birthright of every woman on Earth and there shall be no limits or restrictions on these rituals.

AND it shall be proclaimed as law from the most high that no occasion is too trivial, inconsequential, or unseemly to celebrate with plenty of food and wine. And those occasions shall include job promotions, Pap smears, divorces, blind dates, mortgage payments, and leg shaving.

THE BOOK OF MADGE

WHEN you get older,
I shall forsake you
not. For friends are like
wine—the older, the bet-
ter. You can get equally
drunk with old or new
wine. But intoxication
with old wine is far more
pleasurable.

AND when one of us
discovers we are soon
to become a grandmother,
we shall not receive the
news with denial or defi-
ance but with joy, because
grandchildren are bless-
ings from heaven and can
be given back to their par-
ents when they misbehave
or throw up.

AND we shall buy
funky reading glasses
and call them "cheaters"
so that we might read
lusty romance novels and
the stock page.

AND it will come to pass, that we reach old age, and this will not dishearten but inspire us to lose our inhibitions and do exactly as we please.

AND we will say "Nay!" to the fashion police and wear anything we want, including no-iron pants with elastic waistbands, berets, and sparkly eye shadow. And we shall know that we look fabulous.

FORGET not these words: If your eyesight starts to fail and you leave the house with a great quantity of rouge on your cheeks or lipstick smeared onto your chin, and you look like a sad clown, I will fix your face with a tissue or a wet thumb of my own spittle.

I PROMISE you this: We will lunch at fine restaurants as often as we desire for as long as we can summon the strength to walk into a bistro. And we will eagerly sample new food and old wine, and toast to friendship and loves, lost and found.

A ND we shall eat what we want to eat, regardless of whether it agrees with us or not. For that is why God created Beano.

BE assured: If you decide to take a man for purely lustful reasons, and this man is half your age, but he pleases and satisfies you, I will not judge but rejoice with you and pray that he has a single brother.

BE certain of this: When you suddenly become drenched with perspiration because you have suffered a dreaded hot flash, and you are at a cocktail party and your dress is in danger of becoming soaked, I will accompany you to the restroom and fan you with vigor and provide you with tissues and paper towels until you are dry.

AND when our cycles
stop and our flow
ceases forever, we will not
mourn the milestone as a
loss but rejoice in our
newfound freedom from
tampons and pads with
wings.

AND we will laugh, out loud and long, without embarrassment, no matter where we are in public, and we shall worry not about stress incontinence because that's why God made Depends.

AND we will not look at them as mood swings but opportunities for dramatic expression. And we will not hide our rage, or sorrow, or hysterical joy, no matter how deranged our families fear we have become.

AND we shall shop till we drop, even if this means literally dropping to the earth. For it is better to die shopping than never to have shopped at all.

AND if I am physically able and have a breath left in my body, I will drink wine and dance with wild abandon at your funeral, because I know that's what you would have wanted. And I will wear black. Not because black is the color of grief and mourning. But because black is always in style.